Why can't I swing like a monkey?

T0337165

Written by Julie Penn
Illustrated by Barry Ablett

Collins

What's in this book?

Listen and say 🎧1

forest

arm

back

monkey

tail

leg

Download the audio at www.collins.co.uk/839785

mountain

fur

2 Alice, Mark and Lucy are playing.
Alice can jump.
Mark can climb.

5

Monkeys have got long arms and long legs. They've got long tails, too.

tail

These monkeys are swinging in the trees.
Monkeys can swing very well.

Monkeys find food in the trees.

They eat fruit, leaves and flowers.
Some monkeys eat meat, too.

leaves

flowers

fruit

This monkey has got a nut.
The monkey hits the nut with a rock.
Can the monkey open the nut and get
the food?

rock

nut

Monkeys live with their families
and friends.

This baby monkey is too young to swing. It's riding on its mother's back.

back

These young brothers are playing
a game. They're jumping and climbing.

Now the mother is cleaning her baby.

Monkeys love their families.

Some monkeys live in hot forests.
Some monkeys live in cold mountains.

These monkeys live in the forest.
It's hot here.

forest

These monkeys live in the mountains.
It's cold here.

mountains

The monkeys aren't cold.
They have long fur.

fur

It's night. These monkeys are sleeping.
They sleep in trees.

Lucy says, "Why can't I sleep in a tree like a monkey?"

Picture dictionary

Listen and repeat 🎧³

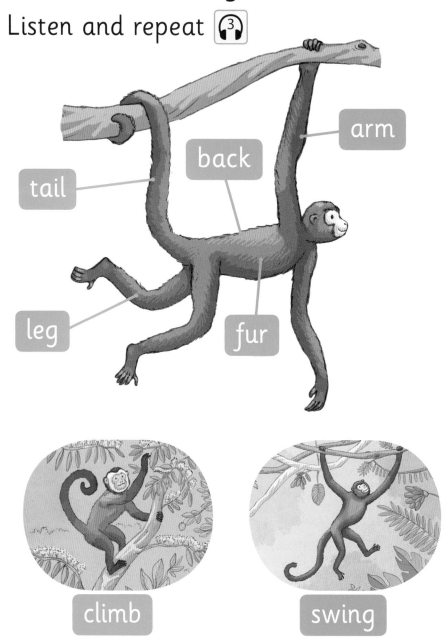

tail

back

arm

leg

fur

climb

swing

After reading

1 Look and match

eating

sleeping

swinging

climbing

2 Listen and say

Collins

Published by Collins
An imprint of HarperCollins*Publishers*
Westerhill Road
Bishopbriggs
Glasgow
G64 2QT

HarperCollins*Publishers*
1st Floor, Watermarque Building
Ringsend Road
Dublin 4
Ireland

William Collins' dream of knowledge for all began with the publication of his first book in 1819.

A self-educated mill worker, he not only enriched millions of lives, but also founded a flourishing publishing house. Today, staying true to this spirit, Collins books are packed with inspiration, innovation and practical expertise. They place you at the centre of a world of possibility and give you exactly what you need to explore it.

© HarperCollins*Publishers* Limited 2020

10 9 8 7 6 5 4 3 2

ISBN 978-0-00-839785-2

Collins® and COBUILD® are registered trademarks of HarperCollins*Publishers* Limited

www.collins.co.uk/elt

British Library Cataloguing in Publication Data

A catalogue record for this publication is available from the British Library.

Author: Julie Penn
Illustrator: Barry Ablett (Beehive)
Series editor: Rebecca Adlard
Publishing manager: Lisa Todd
Product managers: Jennifer Hall and Caroline Green
In-house editor: Alma Puts Keren
Project manager: Emily Hooton
Editor: Deborah Friedland
Proofreaders: Natalie Murray and Michael Lamb
Cover designer: Kevin Robbins
Typesetter: 2Hoots Publishing Services Ltd
Audio produced by id audio, London
Reading guide author: Emma Wilkinson
Production controller: Rachel Weaver
Printed and bound by: GPS Group, Slovenia

Download the audio for this book and a reading guide for parents and teachers at www.collins.co.uk/839785